Language, Logic, and Genre

Language, Logic, and Genre

Papers from the Poetics and Literary Theory Section, Modern Language Association

Edited by
Wallace Martin

Lewisburg
Bucknell University Press

Associated University Presses, Inc.
Cranbury, New Jersey 08512

Library of Congress Cataloging in Publication Data
Main entry under title:

Language, logic, and genre.

    Includes bibliographical references.
    CONTENTS: Fish, S. E.   How ordinary is ordinary
language?—apRoberts, R. Waiting for Gödel: some literary
examples of hierarchical thinking.—Hernadi, P. The scope and
mood of literary works: toward a poetics beyond genre.
    1. Literature—Addresses, essays, lectures.
I. Martin, Wallace, ed. II. Modern Language Association
of America. Poetics and Literary Theory Section.
PN45.L317   801'.9   73-10609
ISBN 0-8387-1446-3

PRINTED IN THE UNITED STATES OF AMERICA

Contents

FOREWORD, Wallace Martin, *University of Toledo*   7

HOW ORDINARY IS ORDINARY LANGUAGE?,
    Stanley E. Fish, *University of California, Berkeley*   13

WAITING FOR GÖDEL: SOME LITERARY EXAMPLES
    OF HIERARCHICAL THINKING, Ruth apRoberts,
    University of California, Riverside   28

THE SCOPE AND MOOD OF LITERARY WORKS: TOWARD
    A POETICS BEYOND GENRE, Paul Hernadi,
    University of Rochester   44

5

Foreword

The three papers here published were read at the meeting of the Poetics and Literary Theory section of the Modern Language Association in 1972. Although not selected with a particular topic in mind, they all concern the shortcomings of conceptual frameworks used in literary analysis. Many of the assumptions that have long governed practical criticism are at present being challenged, and it is symptomatic of the current state of criticism that two of the three essays should discuss its relationship to other disciplines. For after several decades of relative ideational isolation, critics are now discovering new models for literary analysis in anthropology, sociology, linguistics, and philosophy.

The most striking achievements of twentieth-century philosophy and linguistics have been based upon rigorous formalization of theories and methodologies. Linguists set aside the meaning of language in order to discover its formal structure, excluding normative and evaluative considerations in the interest of empirical description. The leading schools of Anglo-American philosophy—logical positivism and linguistic analysis—reduced the concept of meaning to that of formally specified truth-value, or attempted to show, through reference to common usage, that problems about meaning were usually a consequence of odd ways of speaking. Both disciplines focused their attention on "ordinary language" and looked on the language of literature as a derivative or deviant form. Criticism, finding itself separated from areas of the humanities with which it had always been associated, accepted the demarcations suggested by philosophy and linguistics in distinguishing, on the one hand, aesthetics from other domains of human concern and, on the other, literary from ordinary uses of language.

Despite the richness and diversity of recent linguistic studies of literature, the differences that separate linguists and critics have remained essentially unchanged since the publication of Leonard Bloomfield's *Language* in 1933. Stanley E. Fish discussed these differences in "What Is Stylistics and Why Are They Saying Such Terrible Things about It?" (to be published in the English Institute Essays for the year 1972), a paper that might well be read as an introduction to his contribution to this collection. In the latter, "How Ordinary Is Ordinary Language?", Professor Fish argues that a distinction between literature and other uses of language, far from insuring literature's status as a repository of value, leads logically to an impoverished conception of both. The language of literature may not be so different from other uses of language as we once felt compelled to claim. That neither linguists nor critics would unhesitatingly forsake assumptions to which they have long been committed is scarcely surprising. But recent developments in linguistics and philosophy, discussed briefly in the concluding pages of Professor Fish's paper, indicate that these assumptions are now being questioned and that major revisions in linguistic theory are imminent.

Mathematics has always served as a model of deductive rigor for philosophy and the sciences. Our confidence in reason itself is in a pervasive sense associated with the idea that deduction can be complete, coherent, and explicitly formulated. This confidence was shaken in 1931 when Kurt Gödel revealed inherent limitations in the axiomatic method. As Ruth apRoberts points out in her paper "Waiting for Gödel," we must exercise caution when attempting to extrapolate his conclusions to the realm of literature. However, it is evident that a number of literary works call attention to gaps or disparities within their own structure. It is only through reference to another structural level that such disparities can be resolved; and the concept of hierarchy thus seems potentially as important in literature as it is in mathematics, logic, and linguistics. Those interested in the interdisciplinary implications of hierarchy (as distinguished from metasystemic relationships) can refer to *Hierarchical Structures*, ed. L. L. Whyte, A. G. Wilson, and D. Wilson (New York: American Elsevier, 1969), and *The Act of Creation* by Arthur Koestler (New York: Macmillan, 1964).

In the third paper of this collection, "The Scope and Mood of Literary Works," Paul Hernadi reexamines a concept that remains influential in literary criticism despite recent attempts to revise or dislodge it—"the monistic principle underlying most summary classifications of literature into distinct 'kinds.'" In suggesting a more flexible framework of classification, Professor Hernadi looks to painting and music for analogies, calling attention to the generic qualities of the imaginative arts at a time when literature is frequently treated as a use of language subjacent to linguistics or philosophy. This point of view is potentially opposed to that expressed by Professor Fish; but he and Professor Hernadi share an emphasis on theoretical flexibility that would allow varied critical approaches to coexist in tolerant concord.

Stanley E. Fish is an associate professor of English at the University of California, Berkeley. His most recent book, *Self-Consuming Artifacts,* shows that stylistic analysis need not entail the theoretical dilemmas discussed in his paper. Ruth apRoberts is an assistant professor of English at the University of California, Riverside. Her book *The Moral Trollope* was published by the Ohio University Press and by Chatto and Windus in 1971. Paul Hernadi, an associate professor of German and Comparative Literature at the University of Rochester, has discussed twentieth-century conceptions of genre in *Beyond Genre: New Directions in Literary Classification* (Cornell University Press, 1972).

I would like to thank Michael Payne of the Bucknell University Press for facilitating publication of these papers; Robert Scholes, former chairman of the Poetics and Literary Theory section, for his help in selecting them; and Mathilde E. Finch of the Associated University Presses for her editorial assistance.

Wallace Martin

Language, Logic, and Genre

How Ordinary Is Ordinary Language?

Stanley E. Fish

It has been more than twenty years since Harold Whitehall declared that "no criticism can go beyond its linguistics."[1] In that time linguistics itself has undergone a number of revolutions, so that one of the terms in Whitehall's equation has been constantly changing. What has not changed, however, is the formulation of the difficulties involved in any attempt to marry the two disciplines. More often than not these difficulties have found expression in muted declarations of war, which are followed by a series of journalistic skirmishes and then by uneasy, but armed, truces. Linguists resolutely maintain that literature is, after all, language, and that therefore a linguistic description of a text is necessarily relevant to the critical act; critics just as resolutely maintain that linguistic analyses leave out something, and that what they leave out is precisely what constitutes literature. This leads to an attempt, undertaken sometimes by one party,

13

sometimes by the other, to identify the formal properties peculiar to literary texts, an attempt that inevitably fails, when either the properties so identified turn out to be found in texts not considered literary, or when obviously literary texts do not display the specified properties. In the end, neither side has victory, but each can point to the other's failure: the critics have failed to provide an objective criterion for the asserted uniqueness of their subject matter; the linguists have failed to provide the kind of practical demonstration that would support the claims they make for their discipline and its apparatus.

It seems to me that this state of affairs is unlikely to change so long as the debate is conducted in these terms, for what has produced the impasse between the linguists and the critics is not the points they dispute, but the one point on which both parties seem so often to agree. Let me illustrate by juxtaposing two statements. The first is by the linguist Sol Saporta and it was made in 1958 at the Indiana Conference on style:

> Terms like *value, aesthetic purpose,* etc., are apparently an essential part of the methods of most literary criticism, but such terms are not available to linguists. The statements that linguists make will include references to phonemes, stresses, morphemes, syntactical patterns, etc., and their patterned repetition and co-occurrence. It remains to be demonstrated to what extent an analysis of messages based on such features will correlate with that made in terms of value and purpose.[2]

The second statement is dated 1970, and comes to us from the opposite direction. Elias Schwartz, a literary critic, is writing in the pages of *College English:*

> Linguists . . . have failed to distinguish clearly between . . . the structure of language and the structure of literature. . . . From one point of view . . . a work of literature may be regarded as a piece of language. That . . . is the (proper) viewpoint of

linguistics; but as soon as one so regards a literary work, it ceases to *be* a literary work and becomes a piece of language merely. . . . Linguistic analysis is not, cannot be, literary criticism.[3]

Saporta and Schwartz can stand for all of those linguists and critics who have confronted each other in the past twenty years.[4] The linguist says, I have done the job of describing the language; you take it from here. The critic replies, I have no use for what you have done; you have given me at once too little and too much. Superficially, then, the two positions are firmly opposed, but only slightly beneath the surface one finds a crucial area of agreement; in their concern to characterize the properties of literary language, Schwartz and Saporta simply assume a characterization of nonliterary or ordinary language, and that characterization is also a judgment. In Schwartz's statement, the judgment is made with a single word, *merely*—"a literary work . . . ceases to be a literary work and becomes a piece of language merely." Saporta delivers the same judgment indirectly. Terms like *value* and *purpose,* he says, are not available to linguists; what he means, of course, is that they are not available to language. Linguist and critic, then, are united in their decision about what *not* to investigate, and paradoxically, that decision assures that the investigations they subsequently undertake will be fruitless and arid; for if one begins with an impoverished notion of ordinary language, something that is then defined as a deviation from ordinary language will be doubly impoverished. Indeed, it is my contention that the very act of distinguishing between ordinary and literary language, because of what it assumes, leads necessarily to an inadequate account of both; and if I may put the matter aphoristically: *deviation theories always trivialize the norm and therefore trivialize everything else.* (Everyone loses.)

Let us take the two points of the aphorism in order. The trivialization of ordinary language is accomplished as soon as one excludes from its precincts matters of purpose, value, intention, obligation, and so on—everything, in short, that can be characterized as human. What, then, is left to it? The answers to this question are various. For some, the defining constituent of ordinary language is its capacity to carry messages; for others, the structure of language is more or less equated with the structure of logic, and the key phrase is cognitive or propositional meaning; still others hold instrumental views—language is used to refer either to objects in the real world or to ideas in the mind; referential theories are also sometimes representational theories, ranging from the naïve representationalism of so many words to so many things, to more sophisticated philosophical variations. But whatever the definition, two things remain constant: 1) its content is an entity that can be specified independently of human values (it is, in a word, pure) and 2) it therefore creates the need for another entity or system in the context of which human values can claim pride of place. That entity is literature, which becomes by default the respository of everything the definition of language excludes.

At this point, however, something very curious happens. Once you have taken the human values out of the language, and yet designated what remains as the norm, the separated values become valueless, because they have been removed from the normative center. That is to say, every norm is also a morality, and whatever is defined in opposition to it is not merely different, but inferior and inessential. It follows, then, that the area or sphere designated to receive the severed values immediately assumes a peripheral status; and characteristically, those literary critics who work in this tradition are engaged in a frantic effort to find an honorific place for their subject. This then is the first result of the decision to distinguish between ordinary language and literature: both sides of the slash mark lose; ordinary language loses its human content, and literature loses its justification for being because human content has been declared a deviation. The inevitable end of the sequence is to declare human content a deviation from itself, and this is precisely what happens when Louis Milic asserts at the beginning of an article on literary style that "Personality may be thought of as the reverse of humanity."[5] When I first read this statement, I was puzzled by it, as you may be now; but the puzzle is removed as soon as one sees it as the product of an inexorable logic. For if one is committed simultaneously to maintaining ordinary or message-bearing language as a norm and to preserving the link between language and humanity, humanity must be redefined so as to be congruent with the norm you have decided to maintain. In short, humanity must, like ordinary language, be thought of as a mechanism or a formalism, as the reverse of personality, as, and again these are Milic's words, "the uniformity of the human mass." The ultimate confusion involved in this theoretical sleight of hand, of making humanity a deviation from itself, is reflected in Milic's procedures; it is his avowed intention to identify the uniqueness that characterizes an author's style, but he is obliged to regard that uniqueness, when it is discovered, as a regrettable aberration. Thus, for example, Milic's analyses reveal that in Swift's prose connectives often function to suggest a logic the argument does not really possess; he then concludes— an inevitable conclusion, given his assumptions—that this is a tendency of which Swift must have been unaware, for had he been aware of it, it would have been curbed.[6]

I choose Milic for my example only because his statements reveal him to have the courage of his theoretical convictions. Other theorists are less open. Wimsatt and Beardsley, for instance, are engaged in precisely the same operation with their distinctions between explicit and implicit meaning, for in every case it turns out that the implicit meaning is admissible only when it is an extension of explicit meaning; otherwise it becomes an undesirable distraction which is to be deplored even as it is discovered.[7] Wimsatt's stated intention is to rescue style from the category of superficies or scum, but the rescue operation is performed at the expense of the beneficiary, since style is honored only if it makes no claim for itself apart from the conveying of the message.

My intention is not to criticize the work of these men, but to point out the extent to which the decision to separate ordinary and literary language dictates the shape of other decisions even before there is any pressure to make them. A distinction that assumes a normative value at its center is continually posing a choice between that value and anything else, and that choice will reproduce itself at every subsequent stage of the critical process. It reproduces itself preeminently in the only two definitions of literature that are now available, literature as either message plus or message minus. A message-minus definition is one in which the separation of literature from the normative center of ordinary language is celebrated, while in a message-plus definition, literature is reunited with the center by declaring it to be a more effective conveyor of the messages that ordinary language transmits. Of course message-plus theories give the lie to the suggestion (contained in the *rhetoric* of the ordinary language/literary language distinction) that there are two orders of value. In truth, as soon as the distinction has been made and a *norm* has been declared, the values have been reduced to one, and logically the only definition of literature possible is message minus. Message-plus theorists, then, are reacting to an intuition that something undesirable has occurred because of the distinction to which they perversely remain committed. Thus for Michael Riffaterre, to cite just

one example, literature, like language, communicates messages; the difference is that in literature the reception of the
message is assured by literary or stylistic devices whose
function it is to compel attention.[8] This is simply a strong
form of the weaker classical definition of "what oft was
thought, but ne'er so well expressed," where the message
remains at the center surrounded and decorated, as it were,
by verbal patterns that make it more attractive and pleasing.
In a message-minus definition, the priorities are reversed
(these are the *only* possibilities) and preeminence is given
to the verbal patterns; the message is either deemphasized,
as it is in Richard's distinction between scientific and emotive
meaning (that is between ordinary and literary language),
or it is completely overwhelmed, as it is for those who believe
with Jakobson that in poetry, the principle of equivalence
is projected from the axis of selection (lexical content-free
polysemy) into the axis of combination (the channel along
which messages are built up and produced).[9]

What is common to both message-plus and message-minus
definitions are the mechanisms of exclusion each of them in-
escapably sets in motion. Message-minus theorists are forced
to deny literary status to works whose function is in part to
convey information or offer propositions about the real world.
The difficulties and absurdities this leads to are illustrated
by Schwartz's decision to include in the category of literature
"A Modest Proposal," but not Pope's *Essay on Man,* or by
Richard Ohmann's doubt that Elizabeth Barrett Browning's
"How do I love thee" was in fact literature when it was used
to send Robert Browning a message.[10] Message-plus theorists,
on the other hand, are committed to downgrading works in
which the elements of style do not either reflect or support
a propositional core. If there is a clash, declares Beardsley,
there is a fault and it is a logic fault; here again we see the
moral force of the norm of ordinary language, its inevitable

legislation of the ideal of logical clarity, even in contexts that are defined in opposition to that ideal.[11] This hidden morality is even more strikingly operative when Wimsatt asserts flatly that *parataxis*, the absence of sequential relation, is "basically a wrong thing."[12] It is easy to see why message-plus theorists often have difficulty in dealing with works like *The Faerie Queene*, although of course they have the option either of declaring the offending work a failure or of finding a higher message in relation to which the wayward elements can be seen to cohere.

These, however, are the only possibilities, for the choice of either a message-plus or message-minus definition of literature, which is the result of forcing a choice between ordinary and literary language, has built into it an evaluative criterion, the criterion of formal unity. In one context, the criterion is necessary because materials extraneous to the message can be tolerated only so long as they contribute to its expression or reception; in the other, the deemphasizing of the message leads to the requirement that these same materials cohere formally with each other. (What else could they do?) Either everything must converge on a center, or everything must converge in the absence of a center. As always, the alternatives are severely constrained, simultaneously reflecting and reproducing the choice between approving the separation of literature from life or reintegrating it with the impoverished notion of life implicit in the norm of ordinary language. Like everything else in the sequence, the criterion of formal unity is dictated, and it in turn dictates the setting up of a procedure designed to discover and validate it. Every time the procedure succeeds, it not only confers honorific status on a work, but also confirms the explanatory power of the evaluative criterion; and success is inevitable, since only ingenuity limits the ability of the critic to impose unity of either a cognitive or purely formal kind on his materials. (Witness the number of previously discredited works that are admitted into the canon when their "hidden" unity is uncovered.)

My point is not that characterizations of literature as message plus or message minus are inadequate (although I think they are) or that the criterion of formal unity is trivial (although I think it is), but that these and other positions have been determined by a decision that has often not even been consciously made. When Roman Jakobson declares that the chief task of literary theory is to discover "what makes a verbal message a work or art?", whether he knows it or not, he has delivered himself of an answer masquerading as a question.[13] What makes a verbal message a work of art? Whatever it is, it will presumably *not* be what makes it a verbal message. From this covert assumption follows necessarily the succession of entailments I have been describing: the reduction of language to a formal system unattached to human purposes and values; the displacement of those values to a realm that forever after has a questionable status; and the institution of procedures that extend the disastrously narrowing effect of the original distinction into every corner of the critical act. Or, in other words, deviation theories always trivialize the norm and therefore trivialize everything else.

What is the solution? How are we to break out of this impasse? Paradoxically, the answer to these questions lies in the repeated failure of those who have tried to define literary language. What has defeated them time and again is the availability in supposedly normative discourse of the properties they have isolated; and from this they have reluctantly come to the conclusion that there is no such thing as literary language. But to my mind, the evidence points in another direction, to the more interesting, because it is the more liberating, conclusion that there is no such thing as ordinary language, at least in the naïve sense often intended by that term: an abstract formal system, which, in John Searle's words, "is only used incidentally for purposes of human communication."[14] The alternative view would be one in which the purposes and needs of human communication inform language and are constituents of its structure, and it is just such a view that a number of philosophers and linguists have been urging for some time, although literary critics have been characteristically slow to realize its implications.[15] Whatever the outcome of the quarrel between Chomsky and his revisionist pupils, it is clear that the point at dispute between them is the status of semantics, and that in the work of Charles Fillmore, James MacCauley, George Lakoff, and others the semantic component is not something added at a later stage to a fully formed and independent linguistic system, but is a motivating force in that system, influencing syntactic changes as much as syntactic changes influence it. Moreover, this new semantics is not simply a list of usages, or an enumeration of features, but an account of the philosophical, psychological, and moral concepts that are *built into* the language we use (that is to say, the language *we* use). When Fillmore sets out to investigate the "verbs . . . speakers use in speaking about various types of interpersonal relationships involving judgments of worth and responsibility," the relationships and judgments in question are the content of those words, and not the property of an extralinguistic context with which a structure of arbitrary noises interacts.[16] The significance of this is that the language system is not characterized apart from the realm of value and intention, but begins and ends with that realm, and this is even more true of the theory of speech acts as it has been developed by a succession of Oxford philosophers. In this theory, utterances are regarded as instances of purposeful human behavior; that is to say, they refer not to a state of affairs in the real world, but to the commitments and attitudes of those who produce them in the context of specific situations. The strongest contention of the theory is that all utterances are to be so regarded, and the importance of that contention is nicely illustrated by the argument of J. L. Austin's *How to Do Things With Words.* In that book, Austin develops an account of what he calls performatives, acts of speech the performance of which constitutes *doing* something—promising, warning, praising, ordering, greeting, questioning, and so on. These acts are subject to the criterion of felicity or appropriateness and they are opposed to constatives, the class of pure or context-free statements to which one may put the question, Is it true or false. This distinction, however, does not survive Austin's exploration of it, for the conclusion of his book is the discovery that constatives are also speech acts, and that "what we have to study is not the sentence" in its pure or unattached form, but "the issuing of an utterance in a situation" by a human being. The class of exceptions thus swallows the normative class, and as a result the objectively descriptive language unattached to situations and purposes that was traditionally at the center of linguistic philosophy is shown to be a fiction. What takes its place, as Searle has explained, is a "language everywhere permeated with the facts of commitments undertaken and obligations assumed," and it follows then that a description of that language will be inseparable from a description of those commitments and obligations.[17]

In short, what philosophical semantics and the philosophy of speech acts are telling us is that ordinary language is extraordinary because at its heart is precisely that realm of values, intentions, and purposes which is often assumed to be the exclusive property of literature. The significance of this for the relationship between literature and linguistics is enormous. I began by noting the critical objection to equating literature and language—"the literary work becomes a piece of language merely"—but this objection loses much of its force, and the need for distinguishing between literature and language much of its rationale, if the adverb *merely* no longer applies. If deviation theories trivialize the norm and therefore trivialize everything else, a theory that restores human content to language also restores legitimate status to literature by reuniting it with a norm that is no longer trivialized.[18] At a stroke the disastrous consequences of the original distinction are reversed. No longer is the choice one between separating literature from life or reintegrating it with the impoverished notion of life that follows necessarily from an impoverished notion of language. No longer are works denied the designation *literary* by the exigencies which that choice creates. No longer are we bound to procedures that merely confirm and extend the narrowing of options implicit in the original distinction. Possibilities open up; alternatives can be freely explored, and the exploration will be aided by the formal, yet value-laden, characterizations of language that linguistics and linguistic philosophy are making increasingly available. The one disadvantage in all of this is that literature is no longer granted a special status, but since that special status has always been implicitly degrading, this disadvantage is finally literature's greatest gain.

Questions of course remain, and the chief question is, What, after all, *is* literature? Everything I have said in this paper commits me to saying that literature is language, although not, of course, in the demeaning sense with which we began; but it is language around which we have drawn a frame, a frame that indicates a decision to regard with a particular self-consciousness the resources language has always possessed. I am aware that this may sound very much like Jakobson's definition of the poetic function as the "set toward the message," but his set is exclusive and aesthetic—

toward the message *for its own sake*—while my set is toward the message for the sake of the human and moral context all messages necessarily display. What characterizes literature then is not formal properties, but an attitude—always within our power to assume—toward properties that belong by constitutive right to language. (This raises the intriguing possibility that literary language may be the norm, and message-bearing language a device we carve out to perform the special, but certainly not normative, task of imparting information.) Literature is still a category, but it is an open category, not definable by fictionality, or by a disregard of propositional truth, or by a statistical predominance of tropes and figures, but simply by what we decide to put into it. The difference lies not in the language, but in ourselves. Only such a view, I believe, can accommodate and reconcile the two intuitions that have for so long kept linguistic and literary theory apart; the intuition that there *is* a class of literary utterances, and the intuition that any piece of language can become a member of that class.[19]

NOTES

1. "From Linguistics to Criticism," *Kenyon Review* 13 (1951) : 713.

2. "The Application of Linguistics to the Study of Poetic Language," *Style in Language*, ed. Thomas A. Sebeok (New York and London: Technology Press of MIT and John Wiley, 1960), p. 83.

3. "Notes on Linguistics and Literature," *College English* 32 (1970) : 184.

4. For a recent confrontation see the essays by Roger Fowler and F. W. Bateson in *The Languages of Literature* (London: Routledge, 1971), pp. 43–79. See also William Youngren, *Semantics, Linguistics, and Criticism* (New York: Random House, 1972), and T. K. Pratt, "Linguistics, Criticism, and Smollet's *Roderick Random*," *University of Toronto Quarterly* 42 (1972) : 26–39. Youngren and Bateson line up on the Schwartz side, arguing that criticism and linguistics are simply different kinds of activities. Fowler and Pratt, on the other hand, regard it as axiomatic that a connection between the two disciplines exists. The Autumn 1972 issue of *New Literary History* is devoted to a discussion of the language of literature. It includes articles by George Steiner, Richard Ohmann, Paul Ziff, Henryck Markiewicz, and Paul de Man that bear on these questions.

5. "Unconscious Ordering in the Prose of Swift," *The Computer and Literary Style*, ed. Jacob Leed (Kent, Ohio: Kent State University Press, 1966), p. 80.

6. Louis Milic, "Connectives in Swift's Prose Style," *Linguistics and Literary Style*, ed. D. C. Freeman (New York: Holt, Rinehart and Winston, 1970), p. 253. In another article, Milic goes so far as to connect Swift's stylistic habits with his "eventual lunacy": "Rhetorical Choice and Stylistic Option," *Literary Style: A Symposium*, ed. Seymour Chatman (New York: Oxford, 1971), p. 86.

7. W. K. Wimsatt, "Style as Meaning," *Essays on the Language of Literature*, ed. Seymour Chatman and Samuel R. Levin (Boston: Houghton Mifflin, 1967), pp. 370–71; M. C. Beardsley, "The Language of Literature," *ibid.*, p. 290.

8. "Criteria for Style Analysis," *Essays on the Language of Literature*, pp. 414–16.

9. "Closing Statement: Linguistics and Poetics," *Style in Language*, p. 358.

10. Richard Ohmann, "Speech Acts and the Definition of Literature," *Philosophy and Rhetoric* 4 (1971): 15.

11. "Style and Good Style," *Contemporary Essays on Style*, ed. Glen Love and Michael Payne (Glenview, Ill.: Scott, Foresman, 1969), p. 8.

12. *Essays on the Language of Literature*, p. 373.

13. *Style in Language*, p. 350.

14. *New York Review of Books*, 29 June 1972, p. 23.

15. An exception is Richard Ohmann, who in a series of articles has been exploring the significance of speech-act theory for literary criticism. See especially the article cited in n. 10. It seems to me that Ohmann misunderstands speech-act theory and turns it into a system that drives a wedge between ordinary and literary language. See my "What Is Stylistics and Why Are They Saying Such Terrible Things about It?," in *Aspects of Poetics*, ed. Seymour Chatman (New York, 1972). For the work of the philosophical (or generative) semanticists, see *Semantics*, ed. D. Steinberg and L. A. Jakobovits (Cambridge, 1971), pp. 157–482.

16. "Verbs of Judging: An Exercise in Semantic Description," *Studies in Linguistic Semantics*, ed. C. J. Fillmore and D. T. Langendoen (New York: Holt, Rinehart and Winston, 1971), p. 277.

17. J. R. Searle, *Speech Acts* (London and New York: Cambridge University Press, 1969), p. 197.

18. Actually, there is no norm, since rather than a "pure" class of statements (constatives) around which the others are ranged as either appendages or excrescences, we have a continuum of speech acts no one of which can claim primacy. Moreover, these acts are necessarily the "content" of literature just as they are the content of any other form of discourse engaged in by human beings. There is a suggestive point of contact here between speech-act theory and some pronouncements of the structuralist Roland Barthes. Barthes's repeated objections to the "ideology of the referent" is an objection to the claims (for privilege) made by logical denotative language; and when he declares (in *Writing Degree Zero*) that clarity is not a value, but just another rhetorical attribute or (even more provocatively) that meaning is just another style (see *Literary Style: A Symposium*, p. xii), he is doing what Searle and Austin do when they make statements just one among many classes of speech acts. There are, of course, large differences between the Oxford

philosophers and the Structuralists, but they are allied at least in their anti-positivism. In this connection we might note too the practitioners of what has been called "reader-response" criticism, who reject as a goal the extraction from a text of a propositional "nugget" and concentrate instead on the activities of the reader, only *one* of which is the achieving of propositional clarity. See my essay cited in n. 15.

19. One obvious difficulty with this view is that it contains no room for evaluation. It can, however, explain the *fact* of evaluating by pointing out that the formal signals (continually changing and likely to be different in every age) that trigger the "framing process" in the reader are *also* evaluative criteria. That is, they simultaneously *identify* "literature" (by signaling to the reader that he should put on his literary-perceiving set; it is the reader who "makes" literature) and *honor* (validate) the piece of language so identified (i.e., made). Evaluation is thus given a *historical* explanation, an explanation that is isomorphic with the history of tastes, but one that does not touch the question of universal aesthetic criteria.

Waiting For Gödel

Some Literary Examples of Hierarchical Thinking

Ruth apRoberts

Trying to define your self is like trying to bite your own teeth. That is an insight from Eastern religion—and the phrasing is Alan Watts's. It is not a mathematical statement, but it has a remarkably analogous mathematical parallel— in the theorem called Gödel's. And the theorem suggests, I propose, some useful ways of thinking about poetry. Gödel's proof I have to take on faith—and can do so pretty securely, for so far as I can find out it is a proof generally accepted by mathematicians, and indeed generally admired and acclaimed.

You will forgive me if I put the formulation of the theorem in layman's terms, so that I can understand it myself. These I take from J. Van Heijenoort in the Macmillan *Encyclopedia of Philosophy* and from P. W. Bridgman's *The Way Things Are*. The theorem states "that it is impossible to

prove that a logical system at least as complicated as arithmetic contains no concealed contradictions by using only
theorems which are derivable within the system." Conse-
quently: "To prove mathematics free from potential contra-
diction one must use principles outside mathematics, and
then to prove that these new principles do not conceal contradictions one must use new principles beyond them. The
regress has no end—one has languages and meta-languages
without limit." That is Bridgman.[1] In Van Heijenoort's
terms: "Gödel's results . . . establish . . . that mathematics
cannot be formalized in one formal system. Some hierarchy
of systems is necessary. . . . Since mathematics has often
been regarded as the standard of rational knowledge, Gödel's
theorem seems to acquire signifcance for the whole body of
human knowledge." However, he warns us against extending
Gödel's findings: "No doubt these results and other 'limitation'
results have revealed a new and somewhat unexpected situation insofar as formal systems are concerned. But beyond
these precise and almost technical conclusions, they do not
bear an unambiguous philosophical message. In particular
they should not be rashly called upon to establish the primacy
of some act of intuition that would dispense with formalization."

With that word *rashly*, Van Heijenoort seems to be casting
a cold eye upon *us*. But we as literary people do not even have
to be rash: for we can ourselves with something very like
logic demonstrate the limits of our own systems, and the
fact of hierarchy. Because we work with language we are
most especially aware of the limitations of our linguistic
systems. It is Noam Chomsky, taking language as a "central
aspect" of human intelligence, whose recurrent theme is that
the human mind may not be up to understanding how the
human mind works. He himself has, like the mathematicians,
come to something like "limitation results" in a study of

grammar. "Clearly, the rules and principles of this grammar
are not accessible to consciousness in general, though some
undoubtedly are."[2] 'The fact that the mind is a product of
natural laws does not imply that it is equipped to understand these laws. . . ."[3] "A significant gap—more accurately,
a yawning chasm—separates the system of concepts of which
we have a fairly clear grasp, on the one hand, and the
nature of human intelligence, on the other. . . . It is an interesting question whether the functioning and evolution of
human mentality can be accommodated within the framework of physical explanation, as presently conceived, or
whether there are new principles that emerge only at higher
levels of investigation than can now be submitted to physical
investigation."[4] The problem is, as Bridgman says, "The
brain that tries to understand is itself part of the world that
it is trying to understand."[5] Are *we* not often particularly
aware of this, from our study of the staggering complexity
of the way language works in poetry? Do we not sometimes
see how philosophers, logicians even, are embarrassed by
unappreciated inadequacies of the linguistic system? When
we insist on the cultural necessity for knowing a language
other than our native one, it is not because we know the need
to get outside the system, to evaluate it by another system
or systems, to discover thereby the provisional and relative
character of language? And are we not aware of demonstra-
tions in literature itself of the invalidation of systems and of
the efforts to transcend them?

It seems to me that the Book of Job must be the *locus
classicus* of the literary form of Gödel's theorem. If I may
remind you of its structure: There is that folktale framework—the meeting of God and Satan in heaven and a sort of
cosmic wager on whether man can withstand adversity, and
the classical test case: The best of men faced with the worst
and most of calamities. The folktale framework guarantees

our superior, informed position; as *we* see Job stricken and as we attend to the discourse of Job and the comforters, presenting a sample of the ways in which men verbalize the problem of suffering and try to articulate adequate world views, we actually know more than the actors. I think the poet exploits artistically the very naïveté of this folktale, with Satan playing the role of devil's advocate, of all things. Of *course* we know this is not the way things can be, a sort of informal reception in heaven and good-humored discussion with the Unknowable, and *since* we cannot know the way things are—as the whole poem asserts—this banal little fairy tale-myth, legend, suggests how we must *make do* with inadequate, provisional epistemologies. And these may be the means to otherwise unattainable insights, which are themselves valid. How fitting that the folktale framework, beginning and end, is in prose, and the great central main section all in verse! Even though banal then, the framework affords us the detached ironic perspective, and we are by suggestion already *outside the system* of formal logic functioning in the dialogues.

The formal logic of the dialogues is not so naïve or banal. Of the comforters, Eliphaz is the one whose arguments we respect the most, and he is the most sympathetic, but even he fails in sympathy. He reproves Job for cursing the day of his birth, for God is nothing if not just. He, Job, had been so splendid in precept and example when his life was free of calamity, but now "it toucheth thee, and thou art troubled" (4:5). Eliphaz affirms his faith in God's justice, and—in painful irony—asserts "Happy is the man whom God correcteth" (5:17). Job, and we, know that he is not being "corrected"; in fact, *we* know that it is *because* he is innocent that he suffers. His friends cannot believe that he is innocent and he cries out, "Oh that my griefs were thoroughly weighed, and my calamity laid in the balances together" (6:1); and

"To him that is afflicted pity should be shewed from his
friend; but he forsaketh the fear of the Almighty" (6:14).
Job is steadfast in lamenting the injustice and in searching
for an explanation. The friends have shown no understanding.
"Teach me, and I will hold my tongue: and cause me to
understand where I have erred. How forcible are right
words! but what doth your arguing reprove?" (6:25). *I* have
not lost moral judgment; I know iniquity from righteousness.
But Eliphaz denies Job's power to know his own righteousness: "Shall mortal man be more just than God?" (4:17).

Bildad and Zophar are harder trials than Eliphaz. Bildad
is a sort of Polonius, full of traditional proverb and platitude.
To Bildad's conventional morality, virtue-is-rewarded-and-
vice-is-punished, Job counters "How should man be just with
God?"—that is, how should man *make deals* with God. "For
he is not a man as I am that I should answer him and we
should come together in judgment" (9:2). Zophar is the
voice of the theological establishment: God is omniscient
and man is limited: *Therefore,* repent and reform. We see
that none of the comforters can *know* Job's suffering, nor
know his innocence, which two facts invalidate the com-
forter's wisdom, sure though they are of it. The "wisdom of
the race" in Bildad, and religious platitude in Zophar, are
painfully inadequate, yet both are so arrogantly certain,
that Job is driven to sarcasm: "No doubt but ye are the
people, and wisdom shall die with you. But I have understanding as well as you; I am not inferior to you: yea, who
knoweth not such things as these" (12:2–3). And the poet
reaffirms the ironic distance with a technique now considered
very modern, very *dernier cri:* at the very height of crisis
Job cries out, "Oh that my words were now written! oh that
they were printed in a book!" and then the sublime "For
I know that my redeemer liveth" (19:23–25), *redeemer*
we are told being more accurately translated as *vindicator.*

It might be said the *book* the words are printed in, the book as we read it, is the vindicator; and the figure might be interpreted most cautiously as an assertion that man has a sense of ultimate justice.

The contradictions, the paradoxes, the anomalies of this *system* of intellectualizing man's predicament are made cumulatively more obvious and painful, till the poet in a great and memorable moment makes a shift in perspective, and takes us out of that intellectual system into a meta-system. The meta-system has been anticipated in the despairing words of Job himself: "Where shall wisdom be found? and where is the place of understanding? Man knoweth not the price thereof; neither is it found in the land of the living. . . . God understandeth the way thereof, and he knoweth the place thereof" (28:12–23). Job's own arguments, however respectable and noble in their integrity, fail nevertheless in their own logic: for instance, he condemns God's justice, and yet expects to receive ultimate acquittal from Him; he flees God and yet yearns for Him. Job, superior morally and intellectually to the friends, is probably less logical than they. Their positions are more defensible in propositional terms, and yet in the context of the poem we know Job is—if one may say so—*righter*. But all the arguments are canceled by the voice out of the whirlwind:

> Who is this that darkeneth counsel by words without knowledge? Gird up now thy loins like a man; for I will demand of thee, and answer thou me. Where wast thou when I laid the foundations of the earth? declare, if thou hast understanding. Who hath laid the measures thereof, if thou knowest? or who hath stretched the line upon it? Whereupon are the foundations thereof fastened? or who laid the corner stone thereof; when the morning stars sang together, and all the sons of God shouted for joy? (38:2–7)

The meta-system is demonstrated, the ineffable is presented, *in a way*, the way of symbol. The syntax itself, all question now, unanswerable question, symbolizes the departure from discursive logic. One is reminded of Wittgenstein's "Unsayable things do indeed exist" (*Tractatus* 6: 522) and the severe last proposition of the *Tractatus:* "Whereof one cannot speak, thereof one must be silent." Compare Job now: "I will lay mine hand upon my mouth" (40:4). And so must the arithmetician, Gödel says, lay his hand upon his mouth at a certain point. The change is expressed figuratively in Job's statement, "I have heard of thee by the hearing of the ear, but now mine eye seeth thee" (42:5); the *ear* would here symbolize logic, and the eye that more immediate apprehension by which we *see* the limitation of the logical system and *see* by symbol the fact of hierarchy.

But we remember the logicians' warning: Gödel's theorem "should not be rashly called upon to establish the primacy of some act of intuition that would dispense with formalization."[5] True. Mathematicians do still have a discipline. And it seems to me that one of the most moving things about the Book of Job is that it reserves dignity and integrity to the formalization, to man's power of logic. "How forcible are right words!" exclaims Job (6:25). Words *can* be "right." "Though he slay me, yet . . . I will maintain my own ways before him" (13:15). Neither the comforters nor the universe can bully him into saying what he knows is *not true.* He is innocent. There may be something like a concept of original sin in Job, but there is a denial of responsibility for it.

Here is the aspect of Job that has reminded so many of Sophocles' Oedipus.[6] Both Job and Oedipus are as good as man—being human—can be; and both are heroic in maintaining integrity before God and denying culpability. The symbol of *sight* as *insight* that Job concludes with is central to Oedipus along with the Apollo-light imagery. The artistic method is very different, chiefly in respect to dramatic irony. In Job, the superior knowledge of the spectator is only suggested at the beginning, and then as it were suppressed in the body of the work, only to be reconfirmed with the stunning shift into the whirlwind, the primitive outline suddenly illuminated with depth and meaning; whereas in *Oedipus* the double ironic view is insisted on throughout, exploited in every scene and in almost every speech. The irony of the two perspectives in itself implies two systems; and to be aware of two perspectives, two systems, is to recognize the necessity for a yet new perspective that correlates the two. And so the drama, being display, or spectacle, can put before our eyes a kind of paradigm of systems and meta-systems. Kenneth Burke says irony is the perspective of perspectives. The achievement of it immediately grants the existence of hierarchy. And so Job and *Oedipus* work out in something the same way. There is, as Bridgman says of Gödel's implications, "no end—one has languages and meta-languages without limit."

One can always keep moving up the hierarchy until one encounters the Unknowable. Yet it is one of the interesting peculiarities of the psyche (or language) that we can think even about the Unthinkable. Thomas Aquinas perhaps does it with the most elegance and virtuosity, in his definitions of God as what we cannot conceive of. He makes the approach to the limits of human thinking from various directions, and by defining the limits succeeds in a sort of outline or linear silhouette of the Unthinkable. One may not be able to discourse in the meta-language; the point is to conceive of its existence.

But this is very hard to do, abstractly. In our poor anthropological way, we find it much easier to think in terms of characters and stories. And so works like Job and *Oedipus* can make a difficult concept accessible to us. It is a recurrent literary function. A famous and influential instance is that "Dream of Scipio" with which Cicero ends his *De Republica*

by taking us to a vantage point high among the spheres. And
Chaucer makes use of this Ciceronian device in the *Troilus*.
It is another supreme literary moment, when we are taken out
of the system into a meta-system. The ascent into hierarchy
casts a new and different light for Troilus and for us, on
"this litel spot of erthe," and "in himself he lough. . . ."
There is laughter in the last section of Job, too.[7]

Poets discover hierarchy in an endless variety of ways.
Pope even begins the Argument to the *Essay on Man* with
what sounds very like the basic theorem, "That we can judge
only with regard to our *own system*, being ignorant of the
relations of systems and things [Pope's emphasis]." Compare, again, Wittgenstein: "Whereof one cannot speak, thereof
one must be silent." But poets do not stay silent; they depart,
rather, from discursive logic into the area of symbol. Take
Henry Vaughan with the "ring":

> I saw eternity the other night
> Like a great ring of pure and endless light.

The experience is ineffable, and so he reports it in this col-
loquial way, a sort of sublime inadequacy. But what he can
and does do discursively is tell how things look once he has
had that experience, how changed, and then at the end of the
poem he circles back in imitation of the ring itself into a
symbolic statement of the relevance of eternity to us. Wordsworth recognizes the same sort of process in those careful,
beautifully cautious and guarded reports of the "sense sublime of something far more deeply interfused," the "joy of
elevated thought." *Elevated* is a very precise word here, I
think, in the sense of Gödelian hierarchy. Probably Wordsworth's best declaration of meta-system is the climactic symbol
at the end of *The Prelude*, when the climbers who must be ab-
sorbed in finding their footing in the mist and dark of Mount

Snowden emerge at last above the clouds—or *Angst*—into the light of the mountain top, where everything stands clear, and in different terms. The experience is an *emblem*, he says.

Finally I should like to suggest Arnold's *Empedocles on Etna* as the Victorian locus classicus of the Job-Gödel theorem. It is abundantly clear that Empedocles is the victim of over-intellectualization, that enervating "dialogue of the mind with itself," structurally parallel to the philosophical hassles of Job and the comforters, or to the laborious footsteps on Wordsworth's clouded mountainside, or indeed to Milton's devils "in wandering mazes lost." The statement of *Empedocles* is the richer for its two phases: one, the philosopher in society—Empedocles to Pausanias, and two, the philosopher in soliloquy—in each, the "slave of thought." The limitations of human thought, the ways of logic, are Empedocles' theme, his tragedy even:

> We shut our eyes, and muse
> How our own minds are made.
> What springs of thought they use,
> How rightened, how betrayed—
> (I, 327 ff.)

We examine and consider our system and address the gods:

> True science if there is
> It stays in your abodes!

(a very distinct echo of Job) and

> Man's measures cannot mete the immeasurable All.
> (I, 339–41)

> But mind, but thought—
> . . . Keep us prisoners of our consciousness,
> And never let us clasp and feel the All
> But through their forms, and modes, and stifling veils.
> (III, 345–54)

There is much in Arnold's *Empedocles* that is reminiscent of Carlyle, especially in this Gödelian aspect. Arnold's "immeasurable All" is in fact Carlyle's actual phrase in *Sartor*.[8] Remembering Carlyle's mathematical bent, I think he would have liked Gödel's theorem. For it is in a way his one great theme; lacking the proof, he travails with a plenitude of variation to get the message out. And it is as a result of a discrepancy—Carlyle's sure sense of the theorem, and his inability to demonstrate it conclusively—that we have those many loquacious volumes, all, as someone has said, in praise of silence. "Speech is great, but silence is greater." "Logic is good, but it is not the best." There are "things which Logic ought to know that she cannot speak of,"[9] and so, *passim et passim*. He recognized the theme early, in *Characteristics:* "Metaphysics is the attempt of the mind to rise above the mind; to envision and shut in, or as we say, *comprehend* the mind."[10] His recourse to symbol, as explained in the "Symbols" chapter of *Sartor*, becomes, I believe, Arnold's poetic method, most conspicuously perhaps here in his *Empedocles*.

The songs of Callicles, then, interspersed as they are with Empedocles' discourses, function to keep us aware throughout of the song-poetry-symbol mode; and again the two systems imply the meta-system, whose spokesman is at the end Callicles himself, and the last word is a hymn.[11] But Empedocles does not ignobly die: he makes his decision

> Before the sophist-brood hath overlaid
> The last spark of man's consciousness with words. . . .
> (II, 29–30)

And he defends his use of reason:

> I have loved no darkness,
> Sophisticated no truth,
> Nursed no delusion,
> Allowed no fear!
> (II, 400–403)

But the way out of human logic is Callicles' Apollo-hymn at the end. Arnold characteristically links poetry and religion here: the choir is "the nine."

> First hymn they the Father
> Of all things; and then
> The rest of immortals,
> The action of men.
>
> The day in his hotness
> The strife with the palm;
> The night in her silence,
> The stars in their calm.

The end is the Arnoldian ideal of peace, rather than the Hebrew one of cosmic celebration, but the poem has the same structure, I think, as Job. Job was of course enduringly interesting to Arnold, early in his life, and late, and consistently; and the latter's other great biblical favorite, the deutero-Isaiah, which he edited himself, with a sense of its rich symbolism, is acknowledgedly reminiscent of Job.

> For my thoughts are not as your thoughts, neither are your ways my ways, saith the Lord.
>
> (Isaiah 55:8)

Job is so basic to *Empedocles* that one may detect a specific nostalgia for that literary moment "when the morning stars sang together and all the sons of God shouted for joy." It is in the last soliloquy of Empedocles:

> And you, ye stars
> Who slowly begin to marshal,
> As of old, in the fields of heaven,
> Your distant, melancholy lines!
> . . . You too once lived:
> You, too, moved joyfully
> Among august companions,
> In an older world, peopled by Gods,
> In a mightier order,
> The radiant, rejoicing, intelligent Sons of Heaven.

Although the terms are nostalgic, the moment is nevertheless invoked, and the Gödelian theorem is demonstrated again.

Quod erat demonstrandum.

But that is not really the end of the matter; it is not finished. It is, as Gödel shows in the case of arithmetic, *essentially* incomplete.[12] The principle of incompleteness may even seem uncomfortably ubiquitous, and although often nobly demonstrated, can seem commonplace. Take Pascal: the heart has its reasons, which reason cannot know. Obviously. To think about reason at all is to discover its limitations and therefore to impose a new perspective, answerable to our sense of limitation of the single perspective. It is the recurrent function of art to impose the new perspective. Even to paint a Campbell Soup can on a canvas and frame it and put it in an art gallery, makes us look at the subject in a new way, not in the context of What shall I buy? or What shall I have for lunch?, but in the context of What is the nature of this object insofar as it can be determined? "The work of art," declares Wittgenstein, "is the object seen *sub specie aeternitatis.*"[13] But this is still more commonly conceived as the office of religion. To think of God, is, in one sense, to conceive that our ordinary human idea of time and logic is not the only one there is. The spectator at Sophoclean tragedy is said to share the detached view of God, and both *Oedipus* and the Book of Job achieve, at the end, the God-perspective. Something parallel, however humble, is achieved by the Campbell's Soup painting. Lear, when he at last reaches the vantage ground, conceives of becoming *God's spy*. This imposition of the new perspective may be what Arnold intimates as the common ground of religion and poetry.

There is a useful little book by Ernest Nagel and James R. Newman that helps to mediate between Gödel's rigorous world and the world of the layman, and it has some valuable "Concluding Reflections":[14]

> Gödel's proof should not be construed as an invitation to despair or as an excuse for mystery-mongering. The discovery that there are arithmetical truths which cannot be demonstrated formally does not mean that there are truths which are forever incapable of becoming known, or that a "mystic" intuition (radically different in kind and authority from what is generally operative in intellectual advances) must replace cogent proof. . . . It does mean that the resources of the human intellect have not been, and cannot be, fully formalized, and that new principles of demonstration forever await invention and discovery. We have seen that mathematical propositions which cannot be established by formal deduction from a given set of axioms may, nevertheless, be established by "informal" meta-mathematical reasoning. It would be irresponsible to claim that these formally indemonstrable truths established by meta-mathematical arguments are based on nothing better than bare appeals to intuition.

Surely this is very prudently said. There is no reason to despair of our intellects, or to jump the gun in a race after the irrational. Truths we feel to be demonstrable are our ground and security. "How forcible are right words!" Certainly we must be as consistent, as formal, as possible, not permitting those mistakes or solecisms which offend logic. For indeed, the validity of the informal meta-systemic discovery depends on the validity of the precedent formal reasoning that found its own limitation. Pascal's declaration of the claims of the heart is the more valid for his having started in mathematics, even in the probability calculations instigated by the practical exigencies of the gaming tables. Husserl's transcendental has value only for the precedent rigorous striving for the *purity* of his phenomenology. Wordsworth's declaration of the sense-of-something-far-more-deeply-interfused is the more valid for the extreme care in the precedent psychological observations. Arnold's coming to rest in

Callicles' hymn is significant just because, with Empedocles, he has exhausted the possibilities of the "dialogue of the mind with itself." And in the Book of Job, the voice out of the whirlwind is glorious and resonant, in good measure because of the precedent lengthy, widely exploratory, discursive, exhaustive rationalizations of the comforters, notorious in their failure. The Voice is an enfranchisement.

As our terms of discursive logic are perpetually modified by the accumulated total of human experience, by the ever-varying language available, and varieties of individuals in interplay with varieties of cultures, Gödel's theorem would mean, as Nagel and Newman say, that "new principles of demonstration forever await invention and discovery." It indicates, they say, that "the structure and power of the human mind are far more complex and subtle than any non-living machine yet envisaged." And so the office of art, or the office of religion, is never done. New principles of demonstration forever await invention and discovery. And these new principles are not valuable for the softness or "mystery-mongering," but for their precision and specificity. We are right when we value specificity in our poets. Keats, for instance, who so often thinks *new*, writes in a letter:

> I go among the fields and catch a glimpse of a stoat or a field-mouse peeping out of the withered grass—the creature hath a purpose and its eyes are bright with it. . . . Even here though I am myself pursuing the same instinctive course as the veriest human animal you can think of—I am however young writing at random [not *quite!*]—straining at particles of light in the midst of a great darkness—. . . May there not be superior beings amused with any graceful, though instinctive attitude my mind may fall into, as I am entertained with the alertness of a stoat or the anxiety of a deer?
>
> (To George and Georgiana Keats,
> February 14–May 3, 1819)

Gödel's own work, write Nagel and Newman, "is a remarkable

example of complexity and subtlety"—of the human mind. I think the work must be *graceful*, too, in Keats's sense, and bright with precision and intellectual discipline. "It is an occasion," Nagel and Newman conclude, not for dejection, "but for a renewed appreciation of the powers of creative reason." It is an occasion, too, for a renewed appreciation of the powers of the artistic imagination.

NOTES

1. *The Way Things Are* (Cambridge, Mass.: Harvard University Press, 1959), p. 6.
2. Quoted, *Times Literary Supplement*, 15 May 1969, p. 523.
3. *Language and Mind* (New York: Harcourt Brace, 1968), pp. 82–83.
4. *Ibid.*, pp. 5, 83–84.
5. *The Way Things Are*, p. 7.
6. In this discussion of Oedipus I reject the Aristotelian tragic-flaw theory.
7. It is of interest to me to note that Anthony Trollope, in a lesser but distinguished way an ironist like Chaucer, also loves "Scipio's Dream," and appends his own translation of it to his two-volume study of Cicero.
8. See Arnold's *Poems*, ed. Kenneth Allott (London: Longmans Green, 1972), p. 170n.
9. *The Works of Thomas Carlyle* (London: Chapman and Hall, 1896–99), 5: 108 (*Heroes and Hero-Worship*); 28: 6 ("Characteristics"); 5: 26 (*Heroes and Hero-Worship*).
10. *Works*, 28: 27.
11. I ignore here Arnold's argument against *Empedocles* in his 1853 Preface. His critics, from Browning on, have frequently done so.
12. See Ernest Nagel and James R. Newman, *Gödel's Proof* (New York: New York University Press, 1958), p. 86.
13. *Notebooks 1914–1916*, trans. G. E. M. Anscombe (New York: Harper, 1961), p. 83e.
14. *Gödel's Proof*, pp. 98–102.

The Scope and Mood
of Literary Works: Toward
a Poetics beyond Genre

Paul Hernadi

The handy terms *poetry, fiction,* and *drama* may continue to
provide a convenient triad of Freshman English courses for
many years to come. Yet few teachers and perhaps even fewer
of their best students think today that the three pigeonholes
fit such larger birds as Joyces's *Ulysses,* Eliot's *Waste Land,*
or Faulkner's *Requiem for a Nun.*[1] It is, of course, not a
particular doctrine of three (or four or fourteen) genres that
the discerning critic should reject. The fallacy lies in the
monistic principle underlying most summary classifications
of literature into distinct "kinds." Aristotle was more cautious than many later theoreticians of genre in that he pro-
posed a polycentric framework—a set of interrelated

distinctions according to the means, objects, and manner of mimesis. Clearly, there are many respects in which literary works may be similar, and we need several systems of generic coordinates lest we lose our way in the more-than-three-dimensional space of verbal art.

My present attempt to describe different types of scope and mood in imaginative literature must begin by calling attention to an apparent paradox. Every text is limited both in length and in its range of connotation. Yet the imaginative world couched in the limited medium of verbal discourse should impress the reader as a self-sufficient whole without noticeable "gaps" and "edges."[2] In a sense, we expect the literary artist to do what older schools of criticism called improving upon nature rather than simply imitating her: he is to fuse the manageability of the finite with the width and depth of the infinite. As Henry James put it in the preface to *Roderick Hudson:* "Really, universally, relations stop nowhere, and the exquisite problem of the artist is eternally but to draw, by a geometry of his own, the circle in which they shall happily *appear* to do so."[3] In the visual arts, James's magic circle is usually drawn by the painter's or photographer's skillful handling of the relationship between foreground and background. The writer's verbal evocation of imaginative worlds is partly analogous to the mimesis of representational painting. A useful typology of literary scope may thus be based on the relationship between the fore- and background of verbal worlds as they exist in the imagination of an attentive reader.

It is characteristic of lyric poems to go without much background. Who knows or wants to know why Wordsworth decided to cross the Thames in the early morning of September 3, 1802? All we expect and happily receive from his sonnet "Composed upon Westminster Bridge" is the vivid evocation of a mood prevailing in a human mind. Everything

else, even the mind to which the mood can be attributed, remains more or less hidden in the "unlit" background of the
poem. This conspicuous predominance of foreground results
in the evocation of a world with the high intensity of *concentric* tension: our attention is directed to the metaphoric
depth rather than the communicatory width of verbal meaning.
The responsive reader will reenact the poet's mental vision
of "ships, towers, domes, theatres, and temples" as they lie
"silent" and "bare," yet fraught with symbolic significance,
"open unto the fields, and to the sky." The same reader will
hardly make an effort to visualize the ships, towers, domes,
theatres, and temples that Wordsworth actually saw and that
we may find represented in contemporary etchings of London.

Memorable adages neutralize the background from which
their message emerges even more radically. Only because
we cannot conceive of speech without a speaker do we suppose
that someone coined the words "Man proposes, God disposes"
before we could ever hear or read them. But neither the assumed speaker's identity and character, nor the circumstances
of his speech act, invite further exploration. There is, so to
speak, a frame of silence around the "world" of proverbs,
aphorisms, and related literary structures. This frame of
silence turns our attention to the timeless result rather than
the temporal process and interpersonal context of verbal
communication.

Since adages and genuinely lyric poems try to evoke a single
experience emerging from its dim background, the continuous
flux of mental life, they tend to be short and to employ
stylistic devices like rhyme, alliteration, refrain, and meta-
phor. Such devices rely on close interaction between the
words of a text. They demand internal correlation rather
than external elucidation and, as a result, focus the reader's
mind on a single experience as something complete in itself.
The generic scope of adages and poems is thus comparable

to the scope of still lifes, portraits, and self-portraits with a dim and relatively unimportant background. Yet not only adages and poems evoke verbal worlds characterized by concentric tension. Certain kinds of rational and emotive experience lend themselves readily to dramatization. Dramatic allegory, so-called lyric drama (Maeterlinck's and Yeats's one-act plays, for example), and a good deal of the theater of the absurd clearly focus on experienced situation rather than evolving action. Despite their considerable length, plays of this kind tend to be informed by concentric tension; not a unified action but a self-contained experiential response to some aspect of the *conditio humana* provides them with a sense of wholeness and unity.

Most plays, of course, evoke imaginative worlds that are sustained by a solid frame of closely interrelated causes and effects, by the so-called unity of action. The events in works like *Antigone* or *Othello* seem to speed toward a predestined point of final rest as if they were subject to some irresistible *kinetic* law of human action. The tightly knit plot characteristic of most plays and such lesser narratives as anecdotes, fairy tales, and short stories thus conveys a sense of ineluctable causation that makes the worlds of those works emerge as easily detachable segments of the universe. As a result, questions like "How Many Children Had Lady Macbeth?"[4] are often intriguing yet seldom relevant to the critical elucidation of works of this type; we are not really permitted to see beyond the confines of the world Shakespeare's tragedy more or less explicitly evokes. With regard to the visual arts, this type of scope can be likened to a balanced pictorial relationship between fore- and background, that is to say, to the mimetic scope of interior scenes in which the walls of a room or of a cave impose well-defined natural limits upon the viewer's range of vision.

In order to intensify the kinetic tension of their works,

playwrights and short-story writers often compress their imaginative worlds into such small natural units as one family, one day, one city. This explains why neoclassical critics of drama would insist on the famous "unities" of action, time, and place. Yet many great plays and short stories display only one unity—the unity of action—as they focus on a hero's "change of fortune" or one "unheard-of-event" involving a small group of main characters.[5] Such unity of action—the manifest causal interconnection between all significant parts of the evoked world—imparts the suspense of "drama" to a work whether or not it is cast in the dramatic form of dialogue. To be sure, narrative works with the kinetic scope of a streamlined, "dramatic" action often motivate the limitations they impose on the reader's vision by their recourse to first-person narration. Yet there is no obligatory relationship between a certain type of point of view and a certain type of scope or tension. While omniscient narration prevails in most ballads, fairy tales, and many short stories, the world of those works is chiefly informed by a pervasive unity of action.

A third type of cohesive capacity or tension is most conspicuous in the large narrative forms: both the great epic poem and the fully-fledged novel tend to evoke verbal worlds with potentially unobstructed horizons.[6] Yet the same prevalence of vastly inclusive vision over a significant moment of experience or a single line of overpowering action characterizes poems like Pope's *Essay on Man* or Eliot's *Waste Land*, and plays like Goethe's *Faust* or Ibsen's *Peer Gynt* as well. Of course, the limitations inherent in verbal discourse do not cease to operate in those approximations of the totality of human vision. We could compile an endless list of what has been "left out" of the ostensibly total world of such *ecumenic* works as the *Iliad*, *War and Peace*, or the Judeo-Christian Bible. At the same time, each of those "great books" evokes a world with a fully open, potentially infinite mimetic horizon.

The analogy between ecumenic scope in literature and in landscape painting, where the range of the evoked space seems to be determined by the viewer's range of vision, is too obvious to be dwelt upon. But the fundamental difference between kinetic and ecumenic scope in literature may become clearer if we consider that cyclic works tend to evoke more than one "change of fortune" or "unheard-of event." Just as any work with ecumenic tension contains what seems to be sufficient "raw material" for several kinetic plots, the sequential arrangement of a certain number of kinetic works often results in establishing the more inclusive framework of ecumenic vision. The reader of Shakespeare's interrelated history plays, Boccaccio's *Decameron*, or Aeschylus's *Oresteia* trilogy, for example, may gain access to an "ecumenic" view of the world in and through a given series of "kinetic" actions.

Surely, the scope of many works combines aspects of the ecumenic tension of vision, the kinetic tension of action, and the concentric tension of the act of vision. Yet one of those basic types of mimetic cohesion tends to prevail: the mood of most literary works is primarily conveyed either through an intense unit of experience, or through an irreversible process of change, or else through a potentially total view of human existence. Some simplification notwithstanding, it is useful to distinguish three basic moods imparted by works of imaginative literature to responsive readers. These are the mood of fulfillment, the mood of frustration, and the mood of simultaneous fulfillment and frustration. Since most plays focus on a "change of fortune" and contrast a happy or unhappy end to an initially very different situation, the mood emanating from the world of dramatic works is especially pervasive. This is why comedy, tragedy, and tragicomedy have long been privileged to lend their names to classifiers and interpreters of nondramatic literature also.[7] But there is no reason why a proverb, a poem, a fairy tale, or a novel could not convey one of the three moods. Just like plays, those works evoke imaginative worlds in which the reader would either wish or not wish to exist, or else toward which his attitudes are ambivalent.

Let me illustrate these rather broad concepts of tragic, comic, and tragicomic moods by comparing the disparate responses two well-known plays of Shakespeare tend to elicit from readers and audiences alike. Why is the world of *Othello* opposed as something that should not be and the world of *Twelfth Night* welcomed as precisely "what you will"? Because the former frustrates and the latter gratifies the fictive aspirations Shakespeare has led us to endorse. To some extent we may empathize with all characters of imaginative literature, since they are, so to speak, our fellow human beings. At the same time, we have our preferences and gladly exchange a Malvolio's frustration for the happiness of young lovers. We also wish that the frustration of Iago's desires were less belated and thus more complete. Yet Othello's hidden insecurity and misapplied distrust, partly due to his precarious position as an outsider in the social fabric of Venice, counteract the noble Moor's desire for relaxed happiness; it is of Desdemona's adultery, not of her innocence, that he demands and will believe to have received "ocular proof."[8] In other words, the world of *Othello* frustrates the desires with which we strongly identify for reasons more profound than Iago's villainous machinations. This raises the play above the level of sentimental melodrama. Likewise, *Twelfth Night* rises above the level of punitive farce through its emphasis—*not* on Malvolio's petty frustrations but his antagonists' delight in a world designed to grant them eventual happiness. Compared to melodrama and farce, tragedy and comedy can thus be seen as more fully developed, "larger" vehicles of the tragic and the comic mood.[9] Frustration or fulfillment appear accidental in the worlds of melodrama and farce; they emerge as probable, if not indeed necessary, from fully fledged tragedy and comedy.[10]

Clearly, the general atmosphere of frustration or fulfillment can also inform nondramatic works such as Blake's "London" and Tolstoy's *Anna Karenina* on the one hand, Tennyson's "Crossing the Bar" and Fielding's *Tom Jones* on the other. Even adages, or at least a large number of familiar proverbs, may be regarded as fundamentally comic or tragic in this sense of the word. The world implied by the proverb "Where there is a will, there is a way" is totally susceptible to human desires. In the absence of explicit indications to the contrary, we assume that life in such a world is desirable. "Man proposes, God disposes"—the world implied by this no less "valid" proverb is governed by a much more dignified principle than the will of men and women. It is still a world fraught with tragedy for a simple reason: not a cosmic purpose but the experiential reality of human fulfillment or frustration determines the mood of texts with a concentric tension.

Frustration and wish-fulfillment, be it the writer's, the hero's, or the reader's, have attracted much attention in modern criticism. Freud's insistence on the gap between *Wunschprinzip* and *Realitätsprinzip*—between human desires and the potential of the universe to satisfy them—impressed many critics to the point of slighting literary works from which, as the normal way of the world, a sense of lasting human happiness emerges. Another group of critics, including Northrop Frye, would conversely interpret the triumphant end phase of natural and spiritual rebirth myths as suggesting that the ultimate fulfillment of human desires is a higher principle of reality than Freud's austere *Realitätsprinzip*.[11] On strictly literary evidence, I prefer to abstain from taking sides in the seesaw of fulfillment and frustration. To express my view in the myth critic's terms: the "natural cycle" of seasons does not terminate in spring or summer any more than it terminates in fall or winter. Literature as a whole likewise suggests that the very seesaw of births and deaths, pleasure and pain, victory and defeat, fulfillment and frustration is the principle of human reality.

To be sure, individual works often evoke imaginative worlds in which the friction resistance of reality hardly modifies the elemental tendencies of fulfillment and frustration. Yet every instance of imaginative verbal discourse implies the preamble: "Suppose that . . ."; in Sir Philip Sidney's memorable phrase, the poet "nothing affirmes, and therefore never lyeth."[12] Even adages mean what they say in the form of imaginative hypotheses to be verified, as it were, in their own hypothetical context. "Where there is a will, there is a way" is "true" in the world forcefully implied by that proverb. But the same hypothesis of the human imagination can be "falsified" if the frame of imaginative reference is the world implied by another proverb, "Man proposes, God disposes." The following analogy may highlight literature's "noncommittal" way of speaking about desirable and undesirable aspects of reality. Any piece of music composed in a major or minor key relies on the acoustic potential of its particular key (let us say E flat major). The same piece is even more significantly informed by the *kind* of key (major or minor) in which it was composed. Yet the high aesthetic value of the first movement of Beethoven's Fifth Symphony, for example, does not justify a critic's preference for minor pieces at large. Similarly, *King Lear* might be regarded as composed in a tragic key and *The Tempest* as composed in a comic key. Yet our greater admiration for one play or the other would not prove that one of the moods is "more philosophical," more truthful than the other. Indeed, critics preferring tragedies to comedies or comedies to tragedies in general tend to ignore how well a tragic or a comic writer "does his thing." They have decided at the outset that one or the other has a better thing to do.

Beyond doubt, the analogy between musical key and literary mood does not amount to complete parallelism. For example, the major-minor dichotomy prevailed only for about three centuries of Occidental music, yet the polarity of comic and tragic moods seems to provide a more universal frame of reference for the comparative study of literary works. I am indeed suggesting this analogy (just as I was suggesting the analogy between literature and representational painting at the beginning of this paper) as a relatively distant approximation. But I find it rather significant that an inquiry into the nature of verbal worlds should at all permit us to detect correspondences between literature and the other arts. The epistemological implication is hardly doubtful. The verbal medium may well relate imaginative literature to philosophy and other areas of assertive discourse. Yet the fact that literary works evoke imaginative worlds to their readers' minds closely aligns literature and its potential of conveying insight with other arts and their potential of doing so.

To sum up, this paper has been concerned with differences. I have tried to distinguish verbal worlds according to whether they owe their coherence to a concentric, kinetic, or ecumenic tension, and according to whether they impart a tragic, comic, or tragicomic mood to their attentive reader. In other words, I have been suggesting that literary works are mimetic evocations either of a significant experience, or of a unified action, or else of a potentially complete mental vision, and that they tend to convey the mood either of the fulfillment, or of the frustration, or else of the simultaneous fulfillment and frustration of human desires. Yet literary works have many common features, regardless of such differences between them with respect to scope and mood. In the terminology of the present paper, one could describe their foremost shared characteristics by saying that all works of literature are verbal presentations and artistic representations of human action and vision.[13]

NOTES

1. Coherent alternatives to the traditional threefold classification include those suggested in R. S. Crane, ed., *Critics and Criticism* (Chicago: University of Chicago Press, 1952), Northrop Frye, *Anatomy of Criticism* (Princeton: Princeton University Press, 1957), Wolfgang Victor Ruttkowski, *Die literarischen Gattungen* (Bern: Franke Verlag, 1968), Robert Scholes and Carl H. Klaus, *Elements of the Essay* (New York: Oxford, 1969). I offer a critical survey of the books just mentioned and of many others in *Beyond Genre: New Directions in Literary Classification* (Ithaca: Cornell University Press, 1972).

2. Cf. Roman Ingarden, *Das literarische Kunstwerk*, 3rd ed. (Tübingen: Max Niemeyer, 1965), pp. 261ff: § 38: *Die Unbestimmtheitsstellen der dargestellten Gegenstandlichkeiten.*

3. Henry James, *The Art of the Novel: Critical Prefaces* (New York: Scribner's, 1934), p. 5.

4. Cf. L. C. Knights, *How Many Children Had Lady Macbeth?* (Cambridge: G. Fraser, 1933). The title is, of course, ironic.

5. Cf. Aristotle's concept of *metabasis* as described at the end of the seventh chapter of the *Poetics* and Goethe's remarks concerning the proper subject matter for a *Novelle:* "eine unerhörte *Begebenheit*" (Conversation with Eckermann on January 25, 1827).

6. Cf. Georg Lukács, *Die Theorie des Romans*, 3rd ed. (Neuwied: Luchterhand, 1965).

7. Cf. Chaucer on the "manner of Tragedie" at the beginning of the Monk's Tale and Fielding's preface to *Joseph Andrews:* "a comic romance is a comic epic poem in prose."

8. 3. 3.

9. Cf. Northrop Frye, *A Natural Perspective* (New York: Harcourt Brace, 1965), pp. 49f.

10. "Probable or necessary" are Aristotle's words at the end of chapter seven of the *Poetics.*

11. *Ibid.*, pp. 75f. and 123f.

12. *An Apologie for Poetrie.* I quote from J. H. Smith and E. W. Parks, eds., *The Great Critics*, 3rd ed. (New York: Norton, 1967), p. 216.

13. A closer examination of these shared characteristics can be found in my article "Verbal Worlds between Action and Vision: A Theory of the Modes of Poetic Discourse," *College English* 33 (1971): 18–31.